WATCHMAN NEE

The Flow of the Spirit

Living Stream Ministry
Anaheim, CA • www.lsm.org

ISBN 978-1-57593-876-9

Living Stream Ministry
2431 W. La Palma Ave., Anaheim, CA 92801
P. O. Box 2121, Anaheim, CA 92814 USA

10 11 12 13 14 / 7 6 5 4 3 2

THE FLOW OF THE SPIRIT

There is a flow. Before God, we call it the "flow of the Spirit." In every age God insures that this flow is not interrupted, that it is always progressing. The flow of the Spirit is progressing in the churches today. Some time ago I was reading a compilation of Wesley's messages. I thank God because I can see that the flow of the Spirit has moved onward today. If we look back and examine Wesley, on the one hand, we have to admit that his work before God was tremendous and that perhaps our living cannot match his. On the other hand, however, the flow of the Spirit is moving on progressively today.

Here is a basic principle: If we do what God wants to do in our generation, we will get the flow of the Spirit. If, however, we always hold on to our past and demand that God do according to what we rank as important and desirable, we will not get the flow of the Spirit. It was all right to be a Martin Luther in the sixteenth century, but it would be insufficient just to be a

Martin Luther in 1950. It was all right to be a Madame Guyon in the Medieval Age, but it would be insufficient just to be a Madame Guyon in 1950. It was all right to be a Wesley in the eighteenth century, but it is inadequate to be a Wesley in 1950. It was all right to be a Darby in 1828, but it is insufficient to be a Darby in 1950. God is ever pressing onward, and every instrumentality fulfills its function for the church. The flow of the Spirit in the church is always going forward.

Here many people have a basic weakness; that is, they do not recognize the flow of the Spirit in the church. In the church there have been many spiritual giants who have brought about many spiritual things. Today we are heirs to their riches. Saints like Martin Luther, Madame Guyon, John Nelson Darby, Evan Roberts, and Mrs. Penn-Lewis all left us with some spiritual wealth. We cannot thank and praise the Lord enough for this. Yet today even if we should succeed in being a Martin Luther, a Madame Guyon, a Darby, a Roberts, or a Mrs. Penn-Lewis, we would still be a failure because we would not have seen the central point—the flow of the Spirit.

Every age hinges upon a flow. We must admit that the whole trend of the Bible, from Genesis to Revelation, is an onward trend. God has been revealed gradually and even progressively in age after age.

A brother in Hong Kong once asked me the significance of the book of Hebrews. I asked him, "What is the difference between the book of Acts and the book of Hebrews?" The book of Acts is a progressive book. When we get to chapter eight, we cannot go back to chapter two. The Lord had already gone to Samaria. If we go back to Jerusalem, how could we ever get to the uttermost part of the earth? Where the Lord is, there is the way. The Holy Spirit desired to go to Rome, and the Holy Spirit desired to go to the uttermost part of the earth. Going to Samaria was the first step; it was also a preparation for going to the uttermost part of the earth. Producing apostles among the Gentiles was a right and progressive thing to do. After the going out from Jerusalem, it would be wrong to have the desire to stay in Jerusalem. The apostles to the Gentiles kept going until they arrived at Rome.

The book of Hebrews shows us people with one of two identities—either Jew or

Christian, but the book of Acts shows us people with double identities—they were both Jews and Christians. In Acts there was the record of the temple. At that time the Christians still visited the temple on the one hand and prayed in the meeting, "Lord, I consecrate myself to You," on the other hand. When they realized they had sinned, they would seek help from the priest on the one hand and pray on the other hand. At that time Christians divided their time between being Jews and being Christians. There were two sacrifices, two pardons, and two sin offerings. There was the cross, and there was also an animal—the lamb. The book of Hebrews speaks to the Christians who had shrunk back to Judaism: "Are you going to be a Christian, or are you going to be a Jew?" In Acts one could be both a Christian and a Jew, but in Hebrews he could not be both. We must choose to be one of the two. There can be only one redeeming lamb, one priest, and one temple. Therefore, Hebrews 10 says to not abandon the assembling of ourselves together (v. 25). If we stop meeting in Christ, there will be no more sin offering (v. 26). Hence, there is only one basic thought regarding

Hebrews; that is, it is progressive. We must advance. The flow of the Spirit is always going onward.

Since the flow of the Spirit is ever advancing, what was done in Jerusalem would not be sufficient to meet the need in Rome. What was accomplished in Caesarea would not be adequate for today. The advancement spoken of here relates to the entire flow of the Spirit. God let Titus destroy Jerusalem because He could only allow the existence of one Jerusalem. After the church was established on the earth, God destroyed the other Jerusalem. The destruction of Jerusalem brought an end to the sacrifices. Jews might still keep the Passover today, but there is no more lamb. This is progress. God destroyed the first one. In Acts, one could have two identities. But when we come to Hebrews, we can have only one. This is a very serious charge—there is no longer an animal offering for sin.

At the time of Acts, Paul still had a vow (18:18). Please do not measure someone in a particular age according to God's absolute revelation. Today we must follow the flow of the Spirit. Wherever the Spirit goes, we should follow. It was not wrong for Paul to cut his hair and go into the temple to purify himself (21:26), because the flow of the Spirit had reached only to that stage. However, the book of Hebrews tears down the entire Jewish religion. The book of Hebrews says that since that which is perfect has come, Moses is over. God is progressing—in teaching and in the flow of the Spirit.

During the two thousand years of church history, the Spirit of God has been progressing all the time. Even after Acts 28, the Spirit of God is still going onward; He has never stopped. Acts has no ending. We are foolish if we think that the Holy Spirit has left the church. Actually, in every age God has always raised up some people. In every age the church has been progressing. From generation to generation, it is ever moving onward and ever progressing forward, even up to the present day.

Only those who walk according to God's heart are blessed with descendants. Michal bore no children (2 Sam. 6:23), yet Bath-sheba, the mother of Solomon, had sons (12:24). A descendant is the continuation of the line of the Holy Spirit—this is what I call the flow of the Spirit. We have inherited all the grace from our forefathers and ancestors; we receive our spiritual heritage from them. Is God's way an advancing way among us today, or is He moving through somebody else? This is what I call the authority of the Holy Spirit. Once we fail, the Holy Spirit will express Himself through somebody else. The authority of the Holy Spirit is like the trunk of a tree; it grows undeterred. Wherever the seal of the Spirit is, there God's way is.

What if this line is broken? We should study church history to observe God's footprints. Such footprints can be detected in history and in the church. When we look back to Martin Luther, we can see many weaknesses in him, but during his time, Luther's work was the peak of the work of the Holy Spirit. Today we are the fruit of Luther's work. None of us has a life that is long enough to manipulate this line.

Throughout the ages, the church has been like stepping stones in a stream. The work of the Holy Spirit on us is to make us stepping stones through which He can move. This is our greatest glory. If He cannot secure a way through us, He will choose another stone to step on. If He cannot be released through us, we will suffer the greatest loss. The seal of the Holy Spirit may be at a certain place at present, but where it will be ten years from now we cannot tell. Each day the Holy Spirit is bypassing men and setting them aside, group by group. Many people seem to have lost their usefulness. Therefore, we have to be on the path of the Holy Spirit. If the Spirit cannot accomplish anything through us, He must make a new start with somebody else. What a solemn matter this is!

We should always walk on the positive path. In the past twenty years, Brother T. Austin-Sparks has been concerned with the Body service. Some brought up this matter one hundred thirty years earlier, but there was no one walking on this path. The recovery of a certain truth is quite a different thing from actually walking on the path of that truth. It was not until the time of T. Austin-Sparks that this spiritual reality began to manifest itself. Now is the time for us to take the way of fully functioning in the Body service. Everything should be consecrated for the furtherance of the gospel. We attend school for the furtherance of the gospel, and we work for the furtherance of the gospel. The recovery of the Lord in the church is reflected in other areas as well. When the Lord has a move in the church, He makes a corresponding move in the world. We must reach the stage in which the whole Body is coordinating together in the service and the stage in which everything is for the gospel. When the whole church is serving, the Lord's coming will be at hand. At that time not only will teaching be released, but the Holy Spirit will be released as well. The church moves because the Holy Spirit moves first. As soon as the Holy Spirit moves, all will say "Amen" to His move. The Holy Spirit has moved on ahead of us, and we are following Him in this flow. Our words and our spiritual senses should all be up-to-date with the flow of the Spirit.